Students Fired-up over Fun Facts

Students Fired-up over Fun Facts

Making Learning Fun

Jane C. Flinn

ROWMAN & LITTLEFIELD
Lanham • Boulder • New York • London

Published by Rowman & Littlefield
An imprint of The Rowman & Littlefield Publishing Group, Inc.
4501 Forbes Boulevard, Suite 200, Lanham, Maryland 20706
www.rowman.com
6 Tinworth Street, London SE11 5AL, United Kingdom

British Library Cataloguing in Publication Information Available

Library of Congress Cataloging-in-Publication Data
Library of Congress Control Number: 2019949866

∞™ The paper used in this publication meets the minimum requirements of
American National Standard for Information Sciences—Permanence of Paper
for Printed Library Materials, ANSI/NISO Z39.48-1992.

Contents

Contents

Preface

My passion for writing began when I moved with my family from New Jersey to Vero Beach, Florida, as a young child. Writing letters—lots of letters— was the way I stayed in touch with friends and family up North. I enjoyed sharing my thoughts and experiences with others and finding just the right words to express myself.

After graduating from school, while working as a medical transcriptionist and as a court reporter, I continued to hone my writing skills, partly by doing a lot of reading. That unquenchable thirst to read led me to my first trivia book, which happened upon at a local bookstore. I was hooked immediately. I was learning—and I was having fun doing it.

The trivia book made me want to know more. The more I researched, the more I learned—and that led me to combine my fascination with facts with my love for writing into a series of trivia books, including this one.

I wrote this particular book with the goal of engaging students in the learn- ing process, and I knew that required a bit of seriousness, a bit of humor, and a lot of variety. Within these pages, you'll find fun facts and interesting tidbits about a wide range of topics. No matter what you're interested in—be it classic literature, astronomy, fine art, or children's movies—there's truly something for everybody.

Introduction

Where does SpongeBob SquarePants work?
What kind of wood are Jenga blocks made from?
What vitamin do we get from sunlight?

Who says learning can't be fun? This book is full of fun facts, presented in a quiz format, that will have students clamoring to learn more. The multiple-choice, true/false, fill-in-the-blank, and open-ended questions offer information, encourage critical thinking, and provide an opportunity for students to not only test their knowledge of everything from geography to fine arts to science and classic literature but also learn something new along the way.

Special "Did You Know" facts expand on the answers and develop readers' knowledge and understanding of the topic—and arouse their curiosity.

Classroom teachers can use the questions as daily warm-up activities or as a pre-assessment review. They might plan a game show activity around the questions—complete with contestants and prizes—or use the questions/answers as a basis for student research projects.

The book can be a fun learning tool at home as well. Parents and their children can read the book together, taking turns asking and answering questions. They can use the questions and answers as conversation-starters at the dinner table, in the car, or while on a walk.

Hoping to put some fun into your learning? Look no further than the pages of this book.

Happy learning!

CATEGORIES

Kids Classics

Figure 1.1.   Clownfish in its anemone. iStock/Getty Images Plus/oksanavg

1. In the Dr. Seuss book, Myrtle the Turtle was King of the Turtles. True or false?
2. Name the little boy in the Winnie the Pooh stories.
3. In Kipling's *Jungle Book*, what type of creature is Hathi?

   a) Cobra
   b) Bear
   c) Elephant

4. One of the main genres of literature to be performed in a theater setting is _____.

5. In what classic novel can you find the quote: "It's been my experience that you can nearly always enjoy things if you make up your mind firmly that you will"?

6. In "wizard currency," there are five sickles in a galleon. True or false?

7. Who had an encounter with the three bears?

8. How is Scooby-Dum related to Scooby-Doo?

9. What's the color of the man's hat in the classic book *Curious George*?

    a) Yellow
    b) Periwinkle
    c) Chartreuse

10. In the classic nursery rhyme Jack and Jill, Jack fell down and broke what as Jill came tumbling after?

11. From what movie is the quote: "I'll get you, my pretty, and your little dog, too!"

12. Who is the eldest of the four Pevensie children in *The Lion, the Witch, and the Wardrobe*?

    a) Peter
    b) Lucy
    c) Edmund

13. Who laid 514 eggs in Charlotte's web?

14. Mickey Mouse's middle name is Fauntleroy. True or false?

15. In the *Swiss Family Robinson* story, the crew and captain were the only ones remaining on the ship. True or false?

16. On *Sesame Street*, who is the turquoise monster?

    a) Grover
    b) Cookie Monster
    c) Rosita

17. Washington Irving wrote the *Legend of Sleepy Hollow*. True or false?

18. In the animated film *Mary and the Witch's Flower*, what is the name of the strange flower?

19. In the movie *Finding Nemo*, Nemo and his dad, Marlin, are what kind of fish?

20. Name the world's only flying elephant!

21. Six of the seven dwarfs' eyebrows are modeled after what famous filmmaker?

22. The classic *Are You My Mother?* is a story about a baby what?

    a) Chinchilla
    b) Bird
    c) Meerkat

23. The name of what classic block-stacking game is a Swahili term for "build"?

24. Radio Flyer discontinued production of the classic-red wagon during the Great Depression. True or false?

25. Where did SpongeBob SquarePants first go to work?

    a) Slippery Seal
    b) Lackluster Lobster
    c) Krusty Krab

Science

Figure 2.1.   Scientist looking in a microscope. iStock/Getty Images Plus/gorodenkoff

1. Water is hot at 211 degrees Fahrenheit, but at 212 degrees, what change occurs?
2. When dropped, things fall to the ground because of what force?
3. A magnetar has the most powerful "field" in all the universe. What type of field is it?
4. Johannes Kepler, a brilliant astronomer, was the first to discuss how the moon has a profound effect on people. True or false?

5. What is classified into three groups: igneous, sedimentary, and metamorphic?

   a) Fossils
   b) Archaeologists' tools
   c) Rocks

6. Sound travels the slowest through gas. True or false?
7. Which is hotter: the surface of the sun or a bolt of lightning?
8. In what location would you find stalactites and stalagmites?

   a) Circus tents
   b) Caves
   c) Football domes

9. The Goodyear Blimp is filled with nitrogen. True or false?
10. What occupies space in an inflated balloon?
11. Name this basic building block of all organisms.
12. Name this science that was not invented by scientists, but by policemen.

   a) Forensic science
   b) Chemistry
   c) Physics

13. Biology is the study of what?
14. The study of weather is what "ology"?
15. Cu stands for the element Cesium. True or false?
16. This can be a building block of steel or it can help carry oxygen in your blood. What is it?
17. Name this cooking fuel that is produced by heating wood in a low-oxygen environment.
18. Sulfuric is the acid that is found in citrus fruits. True or false?
19. What three letters are an abbreviation for deoxyribonucleic acid?
20. What's a cosmic latte?

   a) Starbuck's latest creation
   b) Cosmic phenomenon that has exactly the same ingredients as in a latte
   c) Color of the universe

21. What is Westerlund 1-26?

   a) A recently discovered object hurtling through space at 250,000 miles a second on a westerly trajectory
   b) A meteorite crater recently found in South Africa that is the largest ever seen on Earth
   c) A red hypergiant star

22. When food is being consumed, chemical reactions are occurring inside the body to break the food down into electricity. True or false?

23. This cannot be created or destroyed; it can only be changed from one form to another, according to Albert Einstein.

24. Do biodegradable products cause harm to the environment?

25. Objects at rest—like a rock, or a bicycle sitting on top of a hill—are examples of kinetic energy. True or false?

Social Studies

Figure 3.1.   Christopher Columbus's ships, the Santa Maria, Nina, and Pinta. iStock/Getty Images Plus/MR1805

1. Eric The Red was a Norwegian Viking and the first European to found a settlement on a bit of land we now call what?
2. Before Columbus made his voyage to America in 1492, what group lived in this land for many thousands of years?
3. What was the use for the Roman hypocaust?

   a) Killing animals
   b) Surgery
   c) Heating villas

4. In 1588, what country sent their famous armada to attack Great Britain?
5. Harriet Tubman helped to free what group?

   a) Slaves
   b) Native Americans
   c) Indentured servants

6. In the Medieval Ages, a jousting competition consisted of two knights charging toward each other and trying to knock the other off their horse with what?
7. In Greek mythology, Zeus was a messenger of the Gods. True or false?
8. Name this period in history that spanned from the fourteenth century to the seventeenth century in Europe.
9. What is the United States of America's highest military decoration?
10. Name this major war that began in 1914.
11. In 1803, the United States purchased 828,000 square miles of land from France. This was called what?
12. Consumer goods such as toasters, washing machines, and vacuum cleaners were being sold during this year because electricity was now in homes.

   a) 1889
   b) 1920
   c) 1934

13. Name this country that has its own style of architecture that includes Doric, Ionic, and Corinthian.
14. A person who is pardoned or forgiven for a crime is granted amnesty. Who makes this decision?

   a) Their mayor
   b) Their lawyer
   c) The government

15. The Agricultural Revolution had to do with the production of medicines. True or false?
16. Name this invention by Roger Bacon that uses a convex lens.
17. Which U.S. president could break a walnut with his thumb and forefinger?
18. In the 1400s, Gutenberg's printing press was developed for printing what?

   a) Maps
   b) Books
   c) Letters and postcards

19. The Battle of Gettysburg was the turning point for the North as the Confederate troops were forced to retreat. What war was this?

20. Neolithic is the period in history when the earth warmed up, the population of animals and humans increased, and the stone was being used for tools. True or false?
21. Monarchy is the type of government that is ruled by a king or queen. True or false?

Physical Education

Figure 4.1. Badminton equipment. iStock/Getty Images Plus/nanoya

1. What exercise class might have you doing a "downward facing dog"?

   a) Yoga
   b) Karate
   c) Tae kwon do

2. Name this sport that involves scaling a very high, steep hill using your hands and feet with a safety rope tied to you.

3. In the 1840s, what sport evolved from the English game of "rounders"?
4. Soccer players wear plastic guards to protect their elbows. True or false?
5. This organ benefits greatly when you are doing an activity that makes your heart pump.

   a) Gall bladder
   b) Pancreas
   c) Brain

6. What is the "flying disc" that is thrown with a flick of the wrist?
7. The Houston Texans football team colors are deep steel _____, battle _____, and liberty _____.
8. In badminton, what can legally touch the net?

   a) Birdie
   b) Racket
   c) Player's left hand

9. How many outs are there in the game of baseball?
10. In what sport do participants use swords?
11. What sport do the Los Angeles Lakers play?

    a) Tennis
    b) Basketball
    c) Curling

12. What sport uses a puck?
13. In the sport of archery, what propels the arrows?
14. Name this sport that involves a rider or performer on horseback.
15. What type of artist was Bruce Lee?

    a) Mosaic artist
    b) Martial artist
    c) Graffiti artist

16. The sport of volleyball was first called "mintonette." True or false?

Technology

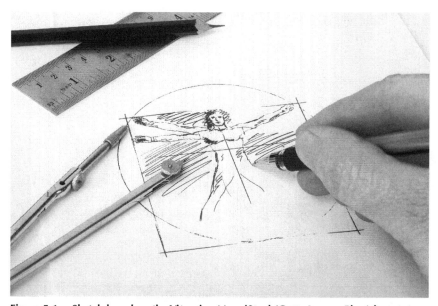

Figure 5.1.   Sketch based on the Vitruvian Man. iStock/Getty Images Plus/charcoa1

1. Once computer files are deleted, they are gone and cannot be recovered. True or false?
2. HTML stands for what?
3. In the first century CE, Heron of Alexandria invented this steam-engine device.
4. Douglas Engelbart created this hand-operated electronic pointing device in 1964.

5. In 1495, which Italian Renaissance genius sketched plans for a humanoid robot?
6. CPU, central processing unit, is the computer's what?

a) Arm
b) Leg
c) Brain

7. Children are using their entire brain when they are interacting with computers. True or false?
8. For twenty years, President Kennedy had an eight-digit code for doing what?
9. NASA exploration of what was established in 1958?
10. In 1958, IC was invented for computers. What does IC stand for?

a) Identity card
b) Incident commander
c) Integrated circuit

11. In the 1800s, Richard Trevithick attached a steam engine to a carriage. What do we call this today?
12. What is the most powerful type of computer?

a) Herculean
b) Super
c) Brawny

13. Oklahoma is the only state that can be typed on the same line of a QWERTY keyboard. True or false?
14. In 1868, Christopher Latham Sholes invented the typewriter and arranged the keys in what type of order?

Language Arts

Figure 6.1.   501671435 "Old Books Horizontally Stacked".

1. In *Gulliver's Travels*, Gulliver is stranded in Lilliput because he was kidnapped. True or false?
2. Identify the adjective in the following sentence: Susie has a great idea.
3. When you are writing and you want to introduce a new idea or a new source, you should start a new _____.
4. If something is identical, it means it is what?

   a) Opposite
   b) Same
   c) Unique

5. Give the word we use to describe two words that are formed to join a new word, as in the newspaper.
6. What is the moral of Aesop's fable "The Ant and the Dove"?
7. What are three punctuation marks you can use to end a sentence?
8. Name the favorite national poet of Scotland.

   a) Robert Burns
   b) Anne Bannerman
   c) Carol Ann Duffy

9. Punctuate the following sentence: Which way is it to the restaurant
10. Poet Homer's works, *The Iliad* and _____, were first memorized instead of being written down.
11. Complete the following idiom: "You can't have your _____ and eat it, too!"
12. An antonym is a word that has an opposite meaning. True or false?
13. Where should an apostrophe be placed: a womans hat.
14. What professional speaks "Aviation English"?
15. What ancient civilization used hieroglyphics to record information?
16. Make the following sentence grammatically correct: The concert will beginning in fifteen minutes.
17. Author John Steinbeck used 300 of these to write *East of Eden*.

    a) Pencils
    b) Pens
    c) Typewriters

18. Graphology studies one's personality and character through their what?

    a) Creativity
    b) Gestures
    c) Handwriting

19. This kind of sentence includes all twenty-six letters of the alphabet.
20. William Shakespeare, the greatest writer of English literature, never attended a university. True or false?
21. If a person is *complaisant*, it means this person is willing to please. True or false?

Geography

Figure 7.1. North America on the globe. E+/Getty Images Plus/tmarvin

1. Arable land is capable of growing what?
2. What state is nicknamed the Land of Lincoln?

   a) Arkansas
   b) Illinois
   c) Montana

3. A peninsula is land that is surrounded by water on all sides. True or false?
4. The United States shares its northern border with what other countries?
5. On what continent is Brazil?
6. The equator and the prime meridian intersect at the Gulf of Mexico. True or false?
7. What major ocean starts with an "I"?
8. Which state is south of Washington?

   a) Idaho
   b) California
   c) Oregon

9. Washington, D.C., is the capital of what country?
10. The Great Salt Lake is in what state?
11. The capital of Colorado is Aspen. True or false?
12. Name this large island in the Indian Ocean that lies off the coast of Africa.
13. Spain borders what country to its west?

    a) France
    b) Germany
    c) Portugal

14. Tectonic plates that move over and under each other form what kind of landmass?
15. What's the largest city in Italy?
16. What is the geological land formation that constitutes a cluster of islands?

    a) Fjord
    b) Archipelago
    c) Isthmus

17. The longest river that is entirely within England is the Severn. True or false?
18. What's the term for a rupture in the crust of the earth that spews lava?
19. Which state is known as the Coyote State?
20. Name the Great Lake that lies entirely within the United States.

Fine Arts

Figure 8.1. Stamp featuring a self-portrait of Rembrandt. iStock/Getty Images Plus/
Andrew_Howe

1. In 1838, Louis Daguerre took the first photograph to be taken of what?

   a) Animal
   b) Human being
   c) Landscape

2. What type of artist was Jackson Pollock?
3. Orange, purple, and green are the three primary colors. True or false?
4. Name the Robert Louis Stevenson novel that tells of the boyhood adventures of Jim Hawkins.
5. The French Horn is an intricately coiled metal tubing ending with a flared what?

   a) Skirt
   b) Bell
   c) Lampshade

6. In an orchestra, there are four families of _____.
7. M.C. Escher's fascinating works of art are based on what?

   a) Anatomy of the human body
   b) Mathematics
   c) Molecular biology

8. What type of artist was Salvador Dali?

   a) Surrealist
   b) Tapestry
   c) Animation

9. Johannes Vermeer's painting "Girl with a Pearl Earring" is referred to as the "Mona Lisa of the South." True or false?
10. What type of artwork depicts inanimate objects such as food and flowers?
11. A trombone is a brass instrument that is played with a keyboard. True or false?
12. During the Middle Ages, the main focus of works of art, literature, music, and theater depicted stories and scenes of what?
13. A musical scale is an octave, which is comprised of how many notes?

    a) 4
    b) 6
    c) 8

14. Seventeenth-century artist Rembrandt painted ninety what?

    a) Horse-and-buggies
    b) Barns
    c) Self-portraits

15. What's the wheel used in pottery that shapes ceramic ware?
16. What kind of art depicts subjects as they appear in real life?
17. Many of Asia's statues are built in honor of Siddhartha Gautama. Who was this "Enlightened One"?

Human Body

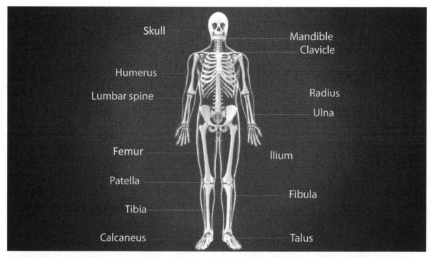

Figure 9.1.   3-D illustration of the human skeleton. iStock/Getty Images Plus/PALMIHELP

1. What's the system in the human body that sends nerve impulses as fast as 328 feet per second?
2. The diaphragm is a long tube that connects our mouth to our stomach. True or false?
3. What organ is used to interpret the light coming into your eyes?
4. Nasopharynx connects what to the mouth?

5. The heart has four what?

   a) Walls
   b) Stairs
   c) Chambers

6. What vitamin do we get from sunlight?
7. Autoimmune diseases occur when the body's own immune system destroys what?
8. Our ears' sole purpose is for hearing. True or false?
9. What is the system called that circulates the blood throughout the body?

   a) Respiratory
   b) Digestive
   c) Circulatory

10. What body fluid is made of plasma, red cells, white cells, and platelets?
11. Spinal fluid provides a cushion for the cortex. Where is the cortex?

    a) Kidneys
    b) Bone in the lower leg
    c) Brain

12. Cellulite is a common infection of the skin. True or false?
13. What pigment that the body produces is the primary determinant of skin color?
14. What sponge-like tissue is located within the bones of the body?
15. Olfactory is the sensory system used for hearing. True or false?
16. Taste buds are located on your tongue, on the roof of the mouth, and in the back of the what?

    a) Nose
    b) Throat
    c) Neck

17. What beats 100,000 times a day?
18. What is the basic unit of all living things?
19. What is the only part of the body that cannot repair itself?
20. Name this important organ that has well over 500 different functions.
21. What's secreted from ducts in the mouth and moistens food for chewing and swallowing?
22. In a human body, there are twelve pairs of bones—the ribs. True or false?

Mélange

Figure 10.1.   Photograph of World's Columbian Exposition (Chicago, USA, 1893).
iStock/Getty Images Plus/ilbusca

1. The metamorph medals in Harry Potter make the wearer turn a bright purple. True or false?
2. Name the natural resource that is being conserved when the paper is recycled.
3. Name this insect with "compound eyes" that begins its life as a destructive force and grows to be the fastest flying insect in the world.
4. What is the significance of "Roundhay Garden Scene"?

   a) It was the first picture film ever made.
   b) It was by far the most stunning, extravagant, intricately designed landscape where many a movie was made.
   c) This most famous garden was depicted in a book for a notorious real-life incident that had occurred in the nineteenth century.

5. In Old English (c. 500–c. 1100), the word "heo" was used to identify people of what gender?
6. What cone made its debut at the 1904 World's Fair in St. Louis?

   a) Traffic cone
   b) Ice cream cone
   c) Pine cone

7. The sundew plant loves to catch the early-morning dew, hence its name. True or false?
8. What punctuation marks should there be in the following sentence: I have never been to Atlanta but Harvey has visited every city in Georgia.
9. What bulb, when cut, will bring tears to your eyes?
10. The stars that are on the United States of America's flag are blue. True or false?
11. How many stages does the life cycle of a frog have?
12. The only continent in the world without any active volcanoes is Africa. True or false?
13. What is the world's best-selling musical instrument?

    a) Ukulele
    b) Guitar
    c) Harmonica

14. In 1941, during World War II, soldiers wanted chocolate that wouldn't melt and was sturdy enough to be carried in their kit bags. Voila! The Kit Kat Bar was born. True or false?
15. What formation do some birds fly in?

16. In the song "All Around the Mulberry Bush," what chased the weasel?

    a) Walrus
    b) Kangaroo
    c) Monkey

17. Name this belt surrounding our solar system where a majority of the asteroids are found.
18. Hydrogen's chemical element symbol is Hg. True or false?
19. The flying fish has to build up what in the water in order to fly?
20. The imaginary line, prime meridian, runs from what two points on a map?
21. Bronze dominated the production of tools and weapons during this period in history.
22. The largest joint in the human body is the hip joint. True or false?

ANSWERS

Kids Classics

Figure 11.1.   Children watching TV, eating popcorn

1. False. Yertle the Turtle was King of the Turtles.

   Did You Know
   Dr. Seuss' full name was Theodor Seuss Geisel, a name he adopted as an undergraduate at Oxford College.

2. Christopher Robin

   Did You Know

   Christopher Robin was named after the author's son, Christopher Robin
   Milne, who was very sick at the time the stories were created.

3. c) Elephant

   Did You Know

   Kipling named this elephant after Hathi, the Hindi word for elephant.

4. Drama

5. *Anne of Green Gables*

   Did You Know

   Famous curmudgeon Mark Twain thought of Anne as the dearest and
   most loveable child in all of fiction.

6. False. There are 17.

   Did You Know

   Galleons are made of gold; they are the most valued coin of the wizard
   currency.

7. Goldilocks

   Did You Know

   The moral of this story centers on thinking about how your actions affect
   others.

8. It's his cousin.

   Did You Know

   Scooby-Dum is a dim-witted Great Dane with buck teeth who longs to
   be a detective.

9. a) Yellow

10. He broke his crown (head).

    Did You Know

    The nursery rhyme continues, although the versions vary: Then up Jack
    got and home did trot, as fast as he could caper. They put him to bed
    and patched his head with vinegar and brown paper.

11. *The Wizard of Oz*

12. a) Peter

13. Charlotte, the barn spider

    Did You Know

    She explains to Wilbur that this egg sac is the finest thing she has ever made.

14. False. That's Donald Duck's middle name.

   Did You Know

   In 1934, Walt Disney overheard Clarence Nash doing his now-famous duck voice for the first time. Nash continued to do the voice of Donald for fifty years.

15. False. The only ones remaining on board the ship were the Robinson family.

16. c) Rosita

   Did You Know

   She hails from Mexico. Her full name is Rosita, la Monstrua de las Cuevas, which translates as Rosita, the monster of the caves.

17. True

   Did You Know

   Irving was an avid reader. He also loved to wander in the misty Hudson River Valley. This area was filled with folklore and served as an inspiration for his writings.

18. Fly-by-night

   Did You Know

   This rare plant blossoms only once every seven years and only in that forest.

19. Clownfish

   Did You Know

   Clownfish live in the sea anemone, as it provides a tentacle-guarded home. This is a mutual relationship, as the clownfish drives off predators that would eat its protector. Clownfish are the only fish in the sea that are not stung by the sea anemone's long tentacles.

20. Dumbo

   Did You Know

   This baby elephant's humongous ears give him the ability to glide through the air. Dumbo was billed as the "Ninth Wonder of the Universe."

21. Walt Disney

   Did You Know

   Happy is the exception, as his eyebrows are white and bushy. It took three years, from 1934 to 1937, to make this movie. Every single frame had to be hand drawn and mistakes were hard to fix; today's animations are computer generated.

22. b) Bird
23. Jenga

Did You Know

These blocks are made from the wood of Alder trees, which grow mainly in the Cascade Mountains. For many years, loggers considered these trees to be weeds and cleared them, using them only as firewood. Lumber companies discovered this wood to be great in building homes and, yes, Jenga blocks!

24. False

Did You Know

Fifteen hundred classic-red wagons rolled off the assembly lines during the Great Depression.

25. c) Krusty Krab

Did You Know

Before Stephen Hillenburg created SpongeBob SquarePants, he was a marine biologist.

Science

Figure 12.1.   Retro revival children . . . making robot in science lab

1. It boils. Guess what comes next? Steam.

Did You Know

As the altitude increases, the atmospheric pressure decreases, allowing the water to boil at lower temperatures. Every 500 feet of increase in altitude causes a drop of one degree in the boiling point.

2. Gravity

   Did You Know
   The pull of gravity varies according to the mass of an object. The weight of an object is variable; its mass is constant.

3. Magnetic

   Did You Know
   A magnetar is a special type of neutron star. The magnet is 20 trillion times stronger than a refrigerator magnet.

4. False. He studied the effect on tides. Galileo Galilei mocked him, saying his theory was unproven.

   Did You Know
   Kepler is the father of modern optics. He developed glasses for near-sightedness and farsightedness.

5. c) Rocks
6. True

   Did You Know
   Sound travels fastest through solids, slower through liquids, and the slowest through gases. Why? Molecules in a solid are spaced closer together, and this causes the sound to travel faster.

7. Bolt of lightning

   Did You Know
   A bolt of lightning can reach a temperature of 53,540 degrees Fahrenheit, whereas the sun's surface temperature is 10,340 degrees Fahrenheit.

8. b) Caves

   Did You Know
   Water that drips in a cave contains lime. Over hundreds of years, the lime builds up and hardens and voila, stalactites are formed.

9. False. It's filled with helium, a gas that is less dense than air.

   Did You Know
   Hydrogen was used in large balloons in the past, but when combined with oxygen, this gas is extremely flammable. A perfect example of this was the Hindenburg, which was filled with hydrogen and burned over New Jersey in 1937.

10. Air

    Did You Know
    Air occupies space and has weight. Anything that has mass also has weight.

11. Cells

    Did You Know

    Cells are the smallest unit of life that functions independently. The invention of the microscope made the study of cells, cell biology, possible. In 1674, Antonie van Leeuwenhoek was the first person to see a live cell with a microscope.

12. a) Forensic science
13. Life
14. Meteorology

    Did You Know

    In 350 BC, Aristotle wrote about meteorology. Meteorologists primarily study the troposphere, as this lowest part of the atmosphere has the greatest influence on weather on the earth's surface.

15. False. It stands for copper.

    Did You Know

    Copper is necessary for the proper functioning of organs in the human body.

16. Iron.

    Did You Know

    Iron in its purest form is found only in fallen meteorites, as it is not present naturally anywhere on Earth.

17. Charcoal

    Did You Know

    Charcoal is mostly pure carbon and it packs more potential energy per ounce than raw wood. Evidence of charcoal production goes back 30,000 years.

18. False. That is citric acid.
19. DNA
20. c) Color of the universe

    Did You Know

    This color was named by a team of astronomers from Johns Hopkins University.

21. c) A red hypergiant star

    Did You Know

    It is one of the largest known stars, having a radius that is 1,500 times larger than our sun. It is located 15,000 light-years from Earth.

22. False. This is energy.
23. Energy
24. No. These products have the ability to break down safely and quickly into natural materials and disappear into the environment.
25. False. These are examples of potential energy.

Social Studies

Figure 13.1.   Portrait of Jean de Bourbon, Duke of Bourbon, mounted in full armor

1. Greenland

   Did You Know
   He named it this, believing "men will desire much the more to go there if
   the land has a good name." This vast wilderness is mostly above the
   Arctic Circle and consists of ice, snow, and rock.

2. Native Americans
3. c) Heating villas

Did You Know

This system circulated hot air under the floor and walls—the closest system to today's central heating.

4. Spain

Did You Know

Spain wanted to dominate Europe and keep Catholicism. England, with their small-maneuverable ships, destroyed the Spanish Armada and changed the course of history.

5. a) Slaves

Did You Know

Harriet was a runaway slave, known as "Moses of Her People." Over the course of ten years, and at great risk to herself, she used the Underground Railroad to lead slaves to freedom.

6. Lances

Did You Know

In the martial game of jousting, the main weapon used was a jousting lance. This long spear-like weapon had a "coronal," which was a crown-shaped metal cap consisting of metal prongs.

7. False. That was Hermes.

Did You Know

The Protector of Travel could move freely and fast between the worlds of mortal and divine.

8. Renaissance

Did You Know

This cultural movement in history started in Italy and then spread to the rest of Europe—a cultural bridge between the Middle Ages and modern history.

9. Medal of Honor

Did You Know

The President of the United States awards this medal to recognize the U.S. military service members whose personal acts of valor go above and beyond the call of duty. These are the bravest of the brave.

10. World War I

    Did You Know

    Although the assassinations of Austria's Archduke Franz Ferdinand Carl
    Ludwig and wife Sophie sparked World War I, there were other fac-
    tors that built up to this war. The four "main" causes of this war are
    remembered by its mnemonic: M-A-I-N which stands for Militarism,
    Alliances, Imperialism, and Nationalism.

11. Louisiana Purchase

    Did You Know

    Many more states were "carved" out of this territory, as it was not just
    the state of Louisiana. Before this purchase, the western boundary of
    the United States was the Mississippi River.

12. b) 1920
13. Greece

    Did You Know

    The Greeks thrives on order and reason, developing categories and
    formal systems called their "orders of architecture" that led to the
    designs of their buildings.

14. c) The government

    Did You Know

    A person who is granted amnesty is free of the conviction.

15. False. It was about farming.
16. Magnifying glass

    Did You Know

    Although Bacon discovered this "glass," optical devices had been used
    for thousands of years. Egyptians used clear pieces of crystal to see
    small objects and Roman Emperor Nero used gemstones, peering at
    faraway actors on stage.

17. George Washington
18. b) Books

    Did You Know

    Gutenberg was a German goldsmith, printer, and publisher and is best
    known for movable type for printing. The Gutenberg Bible, Europe's
    first major-print book, is also known as the "Forty-Two-Line" Bible,
    printed in 1455.

19. The U.S. Civil War
20. True

    Did You Know
    This was also called the New Stone Age, which began in 15,200 BC. No
    one knows for sure why the earth got warmer.

21. True

    Did You Know
    England is an example of a monarchy; the position of king or queen is
    inherited.

Physical Education

Figure 14.1. Girl playing volleyball. iStock/Getty Images Plus/FatCamera

1. a) Yoga

   Did You Know

   Children greatly benefit from yoga in a myriad of ways. It's never too young to start—there's even baby yoga.

2. Mountain climbing

   Did You Know

   This can be a risky activity, as lightning can strike out of a clear blue sky, thunderstorms can quickly form, and avalanches can sweep down mountains.

3. Baseball
4. False. They wear plastic shin guards to protect their shins from kicks by other players.

   Did You Know

   In the 1800s, inmates at London's famed Newgate Prison developed soccer because some criminals didn't have hands, so they wanted a sport in which they could use their feet.

5. c) Brain

   Did You Know

   Activity prepares their brain for learning.

6. Frisbee

   Did You Know

   "Frisbee" originated from the Bridgeport's Frisbie Pie Company in 1871. University students were using metal pie tins as "flying discs." A thrower would shout out "Frisbie" to signal to the catcher to get ready.

7. Blue, red, white
8. a) Birdie

   Did You Know

   The official name for the birdie is shuttlecock, as an earlier version of the game of badminton was called shuttlecock and battledore. The racquets were the battledores. Sixteen feathers are used in making a shuttlecock, and the best ones are made from the left-wing feathers of a goose.

9. Three

10. Fencing

Did You Know

The rapier-style swords used are the foil, epee, and the saber.

Some fencers compete in all three events, but usually, they focus their energies on mastering one weapon. Fencing movements are done so fast that the touches are scored electronically.

11. b) Basketball
12. Hockey

Did You Know

Although exercise is important for children, they should find pleasure and enjoyment with many different sports and activities, as having fun is the ultimate goal. This will lead to a healthy, active adult lifestyle.

13. Bow

Did You Know

During the medieval ages, a skilled longbowman could release twelve arrows per minute; that's an arrow every five seconds! Accuracy of a longbow diminishes over a long distance; nevertheless, a team of bowmen could pelt its enemies with a hailstorm of arrows.

14. Equestrian
15. b) Martial artist

Did You Know

Lee Jun-Fan, professionally known as Bruce Lee, practiced 5,000 punches a day and trained to the "Mission Impossible" theme!

16. True

Did You Know

William G. Morgan was a director at a local YMCA in Holyoke, Massachusetts. In 1895, he invented this sport, wanting an alternative to the physical sport of basketball so that his players didn't have to run.

Technology

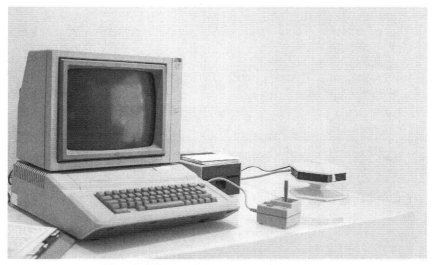

Figure 15.1. Vintage computer. iStock/Getty Images Plus/ficio74

1. False

   Did You Know
   When you delete a file, it really isn't erased as it exists on your hard drive, even if you empty your recycle bin.

2. Hypertext markup language

3. Aeolipile

   Did You Know

   It wasn't until around 1,600 years later that humans would use the same
   steam propulsion technology to power boats and later power all of the
   lights in our homes.

4. Computer mouse

   Did You Know

   In 1960, Engelbart's mouse was a wooden shell covering with two metal
   wheels; they are now made with a plastic shell and a sensor instead
   of a trackball. Many include fancy LEDs displaying a wide variety
   of colors.

5. Leonardo da Vinci

   Did You Know

   Da Vinci's sketch of a mechanical knight was designed to sit, stand, and
   raise its visor. The robot moved with pulleys and cables in place of
   muscles.

6. c) Brain

   Did You Know

   Much like the human brain, the CPU is what makes sense of all the data
   that is being sent to it.

7. False

   Did You Know

   The parts of our brain that are used for reading, writing, concentrating,
   and social interactions are being neglected. Therefore, helping with
   chores, playing games outside with friends, exercising, and reading
   should all be included to stimulate different parts of their brain.

8. Launching U.S. nuclear missiles. The code was 00000000.

9. Space

   Did You Know

   The founding of NASA—the National Aeronautics and Space Administration—
   was a sign that the United States was dedicated in winning the "space
   race" against the Soviet Union.

10. c) Integrated circuit

    Did You Know

    Although all the components were on one chip, the interconnections
    between the components had to be made individually by hand under
    a microscope.

11. Train

12. b) Super

Did You Know

The world's most powerful supercomputer, K from Fujitsu, computes 8.2 quadrillion calculations per second and holds ten times as much information as the human brain. Yet, this "K" needs electricity equivalent to that needed to power 10,000 homes so it's housed in a giant warehouse. The human brain fits nicely inside the human head and operates on the same amount of power as a ten-watt light bulb.

13. False. The state is Alaska.

Did You Know

Alaska is the state with the most volcanoes.

14. Alphabetical

Did You Know

Some of the keys jammed up with this arrangement; therefore, Sholes designed the new universal standard keyboard. U.S. patent number 207,559, issued August 28, 1878, included the QWERTY keyboard—named for the first six letters on the top row.

Language Arts

Figure 16.1.   William Shakespeare. iStock/Getty Images Plus/wynnter

1. False. Lemuel Gulliver survived a harrowing shipwreck.
2. Great is the adjective.

   Did You Know

   An adjective is a part of speech that describes the noun or pronoun.

3. Paragraph
4. b) Same
5. Compound

   Did You Know

   There are three types of compound words: open compounds, which are spelled as two words (post office); closed compounds joined to form a single word (secondhand); and hyphenated compounds, which are two words joined by a hyphen (first-rate).

6. One good turn deserves another.

   Did You Know

   The meaning of this is: A person does a nice act for someone who does a nice act in return.

7. Exclamation point, question mark, period
8. a) Robert Burns, also known as Rabbie Burns, the Bard of Ayrshire
9. Which way is it to the restaurant? (add a question mark)
10. *The Odyssey*

    Did You Know

    Ancient Greeks thought that literature should be presented to an audience and heard, rather than read. For generations, bards memorized Homer's epic poems and recited them to their students.

11. Cake
12. True
13. A woman's hat
14. Pilots

    Did You Know

    Aviation English consists of 300 words, and it is a combination of plain English and professional jargon; this is the "language of the sky" that they all speak.

15. Egyptians

    Did You Know

    This formal writing system combined pictures and symbols, and can be found carved and painted on monuments, temples, and ancient scrolls.

16. The concert will begin in fifteen minutes.
17. a) Pencils

Did You Know

He used up to sixty pencils a day. He said, "It occurs to me that everyone likes or wants to be an eccentric and this is my eccentricity, my pencil trifling. Just the pure luxury of long beautiful pencils charges me with energy and invention."

18. c) Handwriting

Did You Know

A person's handwriting style can give a glimpse into their state of mind and emotions.

19. Pangram. It comes from the Greek: pan = ALL + gramma = LETTER.

Did You Know

An example of a pangram: "The quick brown fox jumps over the lazy dog."

20. True

Did You Know

He dropped out of school at age fourteen and took a job to help the family financially.

21. True. Synonyms are obliging and agreeable.

Geography

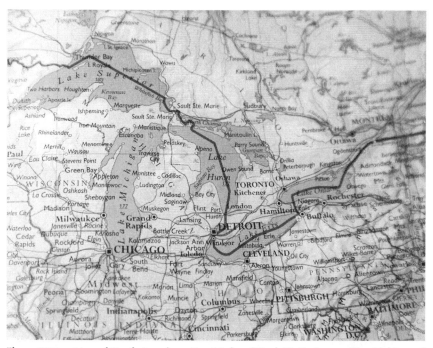

Figure 17.1.   Map of North American Great Lakes. iStock/Getty Images Plus/Lightguard

1. Crops

   Did You Know

   Eleven percent of the earth's surface is used for growing crops. Twenty-seven percent is used for keeping livestock and other food sources.

2. b) Illinois

   Did You Know

   The Illini tribe once lived in the state of Illinois. These Native Americans called themselves Illiniwek, which translates to "best people."

3. False. A peninsula juts out into the water but it is connected to a larger section of land, so it has water on three sides. Florida is an example of a peninsula.

4. Canada

   Did You Know

   This border is known as the International Boundary, and it is the longest international border between two countries in the world, stretching over 5,500 miles.

5. South America

   Did You Know

   Brazil is slightly smaller than the contiguous United States.

6. False. This is the Gulf of Guinea.

   Did You Know

   This Gulf is off the west coast of Africa.

7. Indian

   Did You Know

   This third-largest ocean is bordered by Asia to the north, Africa to the west, Australia to the east, and Antarctica to the south.

8. c) Oregon

   Did You Know

   The Pacific Northwest is famous for its Chinook winds which are warm dry winds that can cause temperatures to reach hurricane strength.

9. The United States

   Did You Know

   D.C. stands for District of Columbia.

10. Utah

    Did You Know

    The name "Utah" comes from the Native American Ute tribe. Other tribes living in this state are the Paiute, Goshute, Shoshone, and Navajo.

11. False. The capital is Denver.

    Did You Know
    This mile-high city was founded in 1858 as a gold-mining town.

12. Madagascar

    Did You Know
    Seventy percent of the nearly 300,000 wildlife species that are on the Island of Madagascar are found nowhere else in the world. Ninety percent of the 14,000 plants that are native to this Island are found nowhere else in the world.

13. c) Portugal

    Did You Know
    Portugal's capital is Lisbon, home to the world's oldest bookstore, Bertrand Bookshop, founded in 1732.

14. Mountains

    Did You Know
    When the plates stop moving, the mountain stops growing and can shrink through a process called erosion. Mount Everest, the world's highest mountain, is still growing! Mount Kea, in Hawaii, is actually taller than Mount Everest, but two-thirds of it is underwater.

15. Rome

    Did You Know
    Every evening, 3,000 euros are swept out of the Trevi Fountain and used to help needy families in Rome.

16. b) Archipelago

    Did You Know
    Archipelagos are often volcanic, forming along mid-ocean ridges. Indonesia has the world's largest archipelago, home to 17,000 islands.

17. False. It is the Thames.

    Did You Know
    The Thames has 214 bridges and more than 20 tunnels crossing it. In 1843, the Thames Tunnel was the world's first underwater tunnel.

18. Volcano

    Did You Know
    Earth's crust is broken into seventeen major, rigid tectonic plates that float on a hotter, softer layer in its mantle. The magma chamber,

below the surface of the earth, releases gases, hot lava, and volcanic ash, erupting into a volcano.

19. South Dakota

Did You Know

South Dakota and Montana are the only two states in the United States that share a land border that is not traversed by a paved road.

20. Lake Michigan

Did You Know

When the last ice age ended thousands of years ago, the glaciers melted, which left the North American continent with five fantastic freshwater lakes.

Fine Arts

Figure 18.1.   Musical instruments. iStock/Getty Images Plus/Leontura

1. b) Human being

Did You Know

This image, of Paris' Boulevard du Temple, required an exposure time of
over ten minutes. Therefore, anything that was moving had disappeared
from the scene: people carriages, etc. The bottom left corner showed a
man who sat still during the shot, as he was getting his shoes shined.

2. Abstract

Did You Know
In 2006, Jackson's abstract painting, No. 5, 1948, sold for an astounding $140 million.

3. False. The primary colors are red, yellow, and blue.

Did You Know
Orange, purple, and green are the secondary colors.

4. *Treasure Island*

Did You Know
Robert Louis Balfour Stevenson's father came from a family of engineers who built many deep-sea lighthouses around Scotland's rocky coast.

5. b) Bell
6. Instruments

Did You Know
The four families are strings, woodwinds, brass, and percussion.

7. b) Mathematics

Did You Know
M.C. Escher failed his high school exams and barely had any formal training in math, yet he enrolled in the Haarlem School for Architecture and Decorative Arts.

8. a) Surrealist

Did You Know
Dali designed the logo for Chupa Chups, Spain's popular lollipop. This eccentric was influenced by Sigmund Freud and explicitly painted the content of his dreams.

9. False. It's referred to as "Mona Lisa of the North."

Did You Know
The reason this painting is compared to Mona Lisa is the girl's curious expression and the mystery that surrounds this painting itself.

10. Still life

Did You Know
The interior of Ancient Egyptian tombs was often adorned with still-life paintings. It was believed that the food and objects in the paintings would become real and be used by the deceased in the afterlife.

11. False. It's played with a slide.

    Did You Know

    Almost all brass instruments have slides; the only one that is played by moving the slide is the trombone.

12. Christianity

    Did You Know

    It wasn't until the Renaissance Era that the religious genre gained a little more *pizzazz* when artists felt the need to express the joy and love of Christianity rather than the bleak and monotonous religious artwork of the Middle Ages.

13. c) 8

    Did You Know

    The "Do Re Mi" song from *The Sound of Music* is actually a good way to teach children how to read and sing musical notes. The notes of the scale correspond to the words from the song: C, D, E, F, G, A, B, C correspond to Do, Re Mi, Fa, So, La, Ti, Do.

14. c) Self-portraits

    Did You Know

    Rembrandt Harmenszoon van Rijn's self-portraits were an important part of his artworks. He is best known for his portraits and biblical scenes using a blend of light and shade.

15. Potter's wheel

    Did You Know

    The earliest known reference to this "wheel" was 2500 BC, shown in Egyptian tombs. Wall paintings in Egyptian tombs show men kneading the clay with their feet, lighting the kiln, and carrying fired pots away in wicker baskets with a wooden yoke spread across their shoulders to spread the heavy weight.

16. Realism

    Did You Know

    This artistic movement rejected romanticism, which had dominated French literature and art.

17. Buddha

    Did You Know

    Buddhism is Asia's major religion and philosophical system, also practiced throughout the world.

Human Body

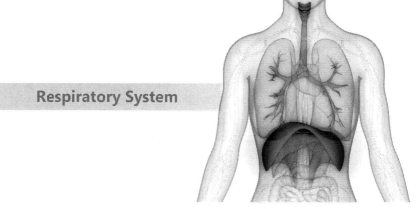

Figure 19.1.   Human respiratory system. iStock/Getty Images Plus/magicmine

1. Nervous system

   Did You Know
   A piece of brain tissue, the size of a grain of sand, contains 100,000
   neurons and one billion synapses, and they all communicate with
   each other.

2. False. This long thin tube is the esophagus, and it attaches the throat
   (pharynx) to the stomach.
3. Brain

   Did You Know
   The brain translates an image into something we can understand.

4. Nose

   Did You Know
   Nasopharynx is the space at the upper part of the throat behind the nose,
   and it allows humans to breathe through their noses.

5. c) Chambers
6. Vitamin D

   Did You Know
   Vitamin D plays a big role in keeping our bones healthy.

7. Healthy cells
8. False. They also help us balance.
9. c) Circulatory

   Did You Know
   This system fights diseases and is responsible for transporting nutrients
   and gases to and from the cells. Also, this system maintains homeo-
   stasis, which is the body's internal temperature.

10. Blood

    Did You Know
    Red blood cells carry oxygen to your cells. White blood cells fight
    germs. Platelets help your blood to clot by forming a "platelet plug."
    Native Americans used blood for paint.

11. c) Brain
12. False. The infection is cellulitis.

    Did You Know
    Cellulite is fat deposits under the skin.

13. Melanin

    Did You Know
    This pigment also gives the hair and eyes their color.

14. Bone marrow

    Did You Know
    Bone marrow has the consistency of thick jelly.

15. False. This system centers on the sense of smell.
16. b) Throat

    Did You Know
    Humans have 10,000 taste buds. The catfish has the most taste buds of
    any animal—more than 100,000. They have them all over their body.

17. Heart

    Did You Know

    Give a tennis ball a good, hard squeeze—you are using about the same amount of force your heart uses to pump blood out to the body. Two thousand gallons of oxygen-rich blood surges through 60,000 miles of blood vessels. That's one colossal task for a fist-sized muscle!

18. Cell
19. Teeth
20. Liver

    Did You Know

    This largest and heaviest internal organ weighs three and a half pounds.

21. Saliva. It is produced by the salivary glands.
22. True

    Did You Know

    The rib cage, also known as the thoracic cage, forms the thorax, which is the chest portion of the body.

Mélange

Figure 20.1.   Soldiers raising the U.S. flag on top a hill. E+/Getty Images Plus/Vincent Shane Hansen

1. False. They turn bright orange.

   Did You Know
   These metals are supposed to be metamorphic, but they are cons. They can also cause the wearer to break out in tentacle-like warts.

2. Trees

   Did You Know
   A ton of recycled paper can save 17 trees, 350 gallons of oil, three cubic yards of landfill space, 4,000 kilowatts of energy, and 7,000 gallons of water.

3. Dragonfly

   Did You Know
   Dragonflies have a 360 vision of their surroundings, seeing all around them at the same time. Great tool for flying!

4. a) It was the first known motion-picture film. (It was shot with a single camera in Roundhay, Leeds, England.)
5. Female

   Did You Know
   Old English, or Anglo-Saxon, is the earliest recorded form of the modern English language; however, the roots of the language are Proto-Germanic, dating back to pre-Roman times.

6. b) Ice cream cone

   Did You Know
   Ernest Hamwi had his waffle booth next to an ice cream vendor who had run short of dishes. Hamwi rolled his waffle into a cone shape to serve the ice cream and the cone was born.

7. False. It likes to catch insects.

   Did You Know
   There's a sweet, sticky fluid on the tiny hairs of this plant's leaves that glisten in the sunlight. Insects think this "dew" is sweet nectar, but they become trapped and cannot free themselves. The leaves digest all of the bugs, leaving only the exoskeleton.

8. Comma before the word "but."
9. Onion

   Did You Know
   Sulfur-containing compounds are released as the onion is cut. These compounds in the onion also cause bad breath.

10. False. They are white.
11. Three stages: egg, larva, and adult.

Did You Know
This process of changing from one form to another is called metamorphosis.

12. False. It's Australia. However, there are a couple of active volcanoes off this continent that are still within Australian territory.
13. c) Harmonica. It's the easiest instrument to play and never needs tuning!

Did You Know
This instrument originated in Europe in the 1800s. In the 1920s, it gained in popularity in the United States with blues music.

14. False. M&M candy-coated chocolates were created.

Did You Know
Frank Mars created these "melt in your mouth, not in your hand" treats during the Spanish Civil War.

15. "V" formation.

Did You Know
This "V" formation creates air turbulence, allowing them to flow off each other's airwaves. In this way, they can fly longer and farther before they need to rest. Every once in a while, the bird in front trades places with one of the birds in the back.

16. c) Monkey. The monkey thought 'twas all in fun. Pop! Goes the weasel.
17. Asteroid belt

Did You Know
This vast doughnut-shaped ring is between Mars and Jupiter. Billions of these irregularly shaped bodies called asteroids or minor planets are gathered in this belt—most are the size of pebbles.

18. False. That's the symbol for mercury.

Did You Know
This chemical was formerly named hydrargyrum, as the Greek word "hydrargyros" means "water" and "silver." It is commonly known as quicksilver, as it looks like silver and moves fast.

19. Speed

Did You Know
Its streamlined torpedo shape helps it to generate enough speed to break the water's surface. Then, it spreads its wing-like fins and is off and soaring!

20. North and south poles

Did You Know

This longitudinal line divides the world into western and eastern hemi-
   spheres, and is the starting point for dividing the earth into its time
   zones.

21. Bronze Age
22. False. It is the knee joint. This hinge-joint is also the most complicated
   joint as it consists of three bones and two joints.

About the Author

Jane C. Flinn, the "Queen of Trivia," is a creative writer from Vero Beach, Florida, and the author of several trivia books, including *The Best Trivia Book Ever.*